The Wild World of Animals

Giraffes

Long-Necked Leaf-Eaters

by Lola M. Schaefer

Consultant:
Anne Warner
Director of Conservation and Education
The Oakland Zoo

Bridgestone Books
an imprint of Capstone Press
Mankato, Minnesota

Bridgestone Books are published by Capstone Press
151 Good Counsel Drive, P.O. Box 669, Mankato, Minnesota 56002
http://www.capstone-press.com

Library of Congress Cataloging-in-Publication Data
Schaefer, Lola M., 1950–
    Giraffes: long-necked leaf-eaters/by Lola M. Schaefer.
    p. cm.—(The wild world of animals)
    Includes bibliographical references (p. 24) and index.
    ISBN 0-7368-0965-1
    1. Giraffe—Juvenile literature. [1. Giraffe.] I. Title. II. Series.
QL737.U56 S33 2002
599.638—dc21   00-012547

Summary: An introduction to giraffes describing their physical characteristics, habitat, young, food, predators, and relationship to people.

Editorial Credits
Erika Mikkelson, editor; Karen Risch, product planning editor; Linda Clavel, cover designer
    and illustrator; Heidi Schoof, photo researcher

Photo Credits
Cheryl A. Ertelt, 4
Craig Brandt, 8
John Shaw/TOM STACK & ASSOCIATES, cover
PhotoDisc, Inc., 1
Robert McCaw, 10
Robin Brandt, 12, 14
Tom & Pat Leeson, 6
Victoria Hurst/TOM STACK & ASSOCIATES, 20
William Bernard, 16, 18

1 2 3 4 5 6 07 06 05 04 03 02

Table of Contents

horns

neck

mouth

tail

tassel

legs

Giraffes

Giraffes have a very long neck. They have two small horns on the top of their head. Giraffes' front legs are longer than their back legs. Giraffes have a long tail with a tassel. Brown spots cover a giraffe's tan body.

tassel

a bunch of thick hair at the end of a giraffe's tail

Giraffes Are Mammals

Giraffes are mammals. Mammals are warm-blooded animals with a backbone. Their body heat stays the same in all temperatures. Female mammals feed milk to their young.

A Giraffe's Habitat

Giraffes live in Africa. Their habitat is wooded savanna. Rain only falls in these grassy areas during two times of the year. Rain helps trees and plants grow. Giraffes eat the leaves of trees and plants to survive.

habitat
the place where
an animal lives

Leaf-Eaters and Water-Sippers

Giraffes are herbivores. Herbivores eat only plants. Giraffes eat bark, twigs, fruit, and leaves. Giraffes need water to live. They receive some water from the leaves they eat. Giraffes sometimes must spread their front legs and bend low to sip from water holes.

A giraffe's tongue is 18 inches (45 centimeters) long. Giraffes use their tongue to pull leaves off tree branches.

How Do Giraffes Eat?

Giraffes swallow their food without chewing it very well. Juices inside their stomach mix with the food. Giraffes later regurgitate this food, or cud, back up into their mouth. They chew it again for about a minute and then finally swallow the cud.

regurgitate

to bring food from the stomach back into the mouth

Mating and Birth

Male giraffes fight each other to mate with a female giraffe. They wrestle by swinging their heavy heads into each other's sides. The male giraffe that wins the fight mates with a female. A young giraffe is born 15 months later.

mate
to join together
to produce young

FUN FACTS

Male giraffes are called bulls. Female giraffes are called cows.

Giraffe Calves

Young giraffes are calves. Calves stand about 6 feet (2 meters) tall at birth. Newborn calves weigh nearly 150 pounds (70 kilograms) at birth. Calves drink milk from their mothers until they are about 1 year old.

Predators

Few animals can kill giraffes because of giraffes' large size. Lions, leopards, and hyenas sometimes attack giraffes. Giraffes run away from these predators. Some giraffes run up to 35 miles (56 kilometers) per hour. Giraffes also kick predators with their feet.

Giraffes and People

People can protect giraffes' habitat. People often take over the land where giraffes live. They build houses and farm on the land. Some people have set up parks where giraffes can live. Giraffes have space to live and food to eat in these protected areas.

Hands On: Reach for the Trees

A giraffe's long neck helps it reach the leaves and fruit on a tree's highest branches. A giraffe's food usually hangs 14 to 17 feet (4 to 5 meters) above the ground. Try this activity to see if you can reach as high as a giraffe can.

What You Need

A tall tree with leaves
An adult
Tape measure
Paper

Pen
4 yardsticks
Masking tape

What You Do

1. Find a tall tree outside. Stretch your right hand above your head. Can you touch the tree's branches?
2. Have an adult measure from the ground to the top of your right hand.
3. Record how tall you are with your arm raised.
4. Overlap two yardsticks by 3 inches (7.6 centimeters) and tape them together.
5. Continue taping the yardsticks together until you have one long stick. How long are the four sticks taped together?
6. Add the measurement from step 5 to the measurement you wrote down in step 3. The number you get from adding the two measurements is about the height of most giraffes.
7. Raise the yardsticks as high as you can above your head. The tip of your yardstick reaches as high as some giraffes' heads. Other animals cannot reach as high as a giraffe can. A giraffe's food is safe at the top of a tree.

Words to Know

grassland (GRASS-land)—a large open area of grass

herbivore (HUR-buh-vor)—an animal that eats only plants

mammal (MAM-uhl)—a warm-blooded animal that has a backbone; female mammals feed milk to their young.

pattern (PAT-urn)—a repeating order of colors, shapes, or figures; giraffes have a pattern of brown spots on their bodies.

predator (PRED-uh-tur)—an animal that hunts and kills other animals for food

warm-blooded (warm-BLUHD-id)—having a body temperature that stays the same

Read More

Johnston, Marianne. *Giraffes and Their Babies.* A Zoo Life Book. New York: PowerKids Press, 1999.

Kalman, Bobbie, and Greg Nickles. *Giraffes.* Crabapples. New York: Crabtree Publishing, 1997.

Markert, Jenny. *Giraffes.* Chanhassen, Minn.: Child's World, 2001.

Internet Sites

Africa: Reticulated Giraffe
http://www.oaklandzoo.org/atoz/azgiraf.html
Giraffe Printout
http://www.EnchantedLearning.com/subjects/mammals/giraffe/
    Giraffecoloring.shtml
Planet Giraffe
http://www.planet-pets.com/plntgraf.htm

Index